IMAGES
of America

HILTON HEAD ISLAND

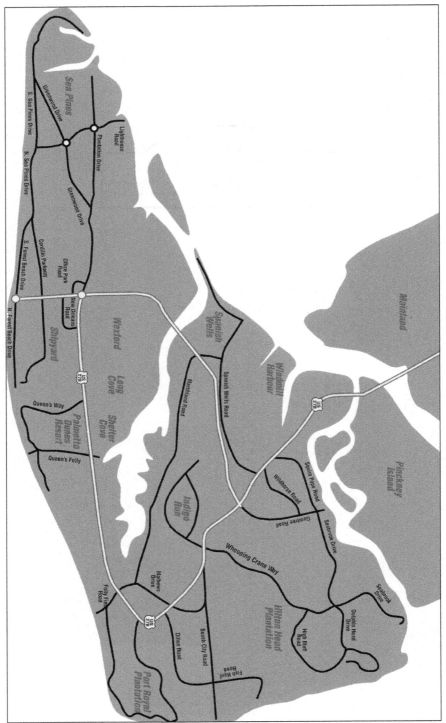

This map shows the modern-day plantations and major roads of Hilton Head Island. (Frey Media/TriComm Productions/the Resort Channel 60.)

IMAGES
of America

HILTON HEAD ISLAND

Coastal Discovery Museum
Hilton Head Island

Natalie Hefter, Editor
History Coordinator

ARCADIA
PUBLISHING

Published by Arcadia Publishing,
Charleston, South Carolina

Library of Congress Catalog Card Number: 98-88303

For all general information contact Arcadia Publishing at:
Telephone 843-853-2070
Fax 843-853-0044
E-mail: sales@arcadiapublishing.com
For customer service and orders:
Toll-Free 1-888-313-2665

Visit us on the Internet at www.arcadiapublishing.com

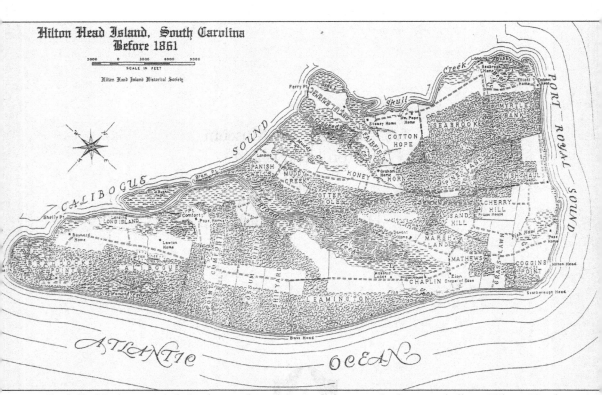

Fred C. Hack compiled deed records to create this map of what antebellum Hilton Head properties were named. Some names like Shipyard, Leamington, Honey Horn, Calibogue, and others are used today. (Hilton Head Historical Society.)

CONTENTS

ACKNOWLEDGMENTS

Hilton Head Island is a project of the Coastal Discovery Museum, the Environmental and Historical Museum on Hilton Head Island. The purpose of this book is to present a chronological outline of area history as reflected in the photographs and illustrations from the collections of the museum and many community residents, businesses, and organizations. There are many other photographs and resources yet to be published or displayed. Please visit the Coastal Discovery Museum to learn more through our exhibits, live and televised programs, and tours of the area's historical sites.

We wish to thank the following people, businesses, and organizations for their contributions and support of *Hilton Head Island*.

The following individuals and families lent photographs which were included in the book: Ned McNair, Abe Grant, Evelyn Mitchell, Barbara Hudson, Joe Pinckney, Ben Stewart, Elizabeth Grant, Elaine Kennedy, Lamar Priester Jr., Betty Ann Thompson Comer, Ed Wiggins Sr., Delores Lawyer, Greg Smith, Ernest Ferguson, Capin family, Hack family, Phillip Propst family, Tommy Heyward, Frances Baker, Dana Palmer, June Eggert, Sue and Bob Wiener, Elrid Moody, Marian Broome, Mary Ann Peeples, Betty Lightfoot, Gretchen Freund, and Sandy Painter, and Mose Hudson family.

Many businesses and organizations searched their archives as well. They are Western Reserve Historical Society, Adventure Inn, the *Island Packet*, the Library of Congress, Parris Island Museum, First Presbyterian Church, Frey Media, Ed Pinckney and Associates, Hilton Head Island Chamber of Commerce, the Westin Resort, Crowne Plaza, Marriott Grande Ocean, Disney's Hilton Head Island Resort, Palmetto Electric Cooperative, Hilton Head Island Medical Center and Clinics, Self Family Arts Center, Island Rentals and Real Estate, Technical College of the Low Country, and the Hilton Head Historical Society. Dozens of other organizations, individuals, and businesses submitted photographs which we did not have room for in this volume.

Without the help of many others, the technical aspect of this book, reproducing photos, scanning the images, and enhancing the images could never have been completed. Thanks to Ken Mak for duplicating images and scanning slides; Chris Hefter, Angie Coyle, and Robert Highsmith for computer help at Optimum Resource; Greg DeWitt for scanning and helping with layout; Pro Photo and Coligny One Hour Photo for developing and scanning; Charles Grace at Meissner Illustrated for emergency scanning; and Hilton Head Island Middle School for loaning a computer for us to use with a scanner.

Several other people played important parts in putting the book together. Sue Winter and Sue Tritschler helped get the project started, Beth Patton and Sara Borton at the *Island Packet* opened the paper's archives to us, and the Fred and Billie Hack and Mose Hudson families were especially helpful in bringing both families' experiences to life for us. Editorial assistance was provided by Kim Washok, Inas Otten, and Delores Lawyer. Chris Hefter helped with photo selection and layout. Elaine Rothschild tirelessly followed up on research, organized a great deal of information, and provided support in the final days. Richard Hefter and Evelyn Mallick helped with copy editing and content suggestions. Carol Kruzelock, Robert McFee, Isaac Wilborn, the Georgia Historical Society, and Fran Marscher helped with clarifying information.

For over a year, the museum has collected information for the timeline which follows. Many islanders contributed information, but several individuals need to be recognized for their significant contributions to this document. They are Rev. Robert Peeples, Johnnie Mitchell, George Stidworthy, Bill Slaughter, Ben Racusin, Chris Judge, Carolyn Grant, Margaret Greer, and Sally Krebs of the Town of Hilton Head.

As a non-profit museum, there are several organizations which should be recognized for their financial support for this project. The Hilton Head Island Foundation funded Natalie's position during the project. The MCI Heritage Foundation donated funds for this book to be turned into an exhibit in the museum. Hargray Communications, the Bargain Box, and Palmetto Electric Cooperative Trust are longtime donors to the museum and provide much needed support throughout the year. Special thanks also go to the Town of Hilton Head Island for its support of the museum's programs.

The Coastal Discovery Museum is located at 100 William Hilton Parkway on the north end of Hilton Head at Mile Marker #1. The mailing address is P.O. Box 23497, Hilton Head Island, SC 29925. The museum is open year round, seven days a week from 9 a.m. to 5 p.m. The telephone number is (843) 689-6767; the web page address is *http://www.hhisland.com /hiltonhead/museum.html*.

INTRODUCTION

Hilton Head Island's history dates back thousands of years to its geographic formation and its Native American occupation. This book, however, documents the island's more recent past through the viewfinder of the camera.

The following timeline is a chronology compiled by the Coastal Discovery Museum. It traces the island's history from its beginning to the present day. It addresses the early history which cannot be shown in photographs and provides additional information about the more recent past that could not be shared in the chapters that follow. No timeline could ever be absolutely complete, but it marks the beginning of documenting and recording the island's history in print. Our thanks go to the dozens of editors who helped create the timeline.

Chris Tenne Pendleton, Executive Director, Coastal Discovery Museum
Natalie Harvey, History Coordinator, Coastal Discovery Museum

TIMELINE OF
HILTON HEAD ISLAND

Geologic Formation and Pre-History
450 Million Years ago–4,000 years ago

450 million years ago	The sea level was 400 feet higher than today. The coast was near present-day Columbia, South Carolina.
50,000 years ago	This area's sea level was 15 feet higher than it is today. Only a few ridges were above the sea level.
40,000 years ago	Glacial activity caused the sea level to fall all over the world. Small islands were visible above the sea level in this area.
15,000 years ago today.	The sea level was at its lowest point, 400 feet below where it is
4,000 years ago	The sea level had risen to near its present level. This island closely resembled its current appearance.

Native American Occupation
8000 B.C.–1500 A.D.

8000 B.C. (10,000 years ago)	Paleo-Indians occupied this area 5,000 years before the Egyptian pyramids were built. They hunted prehistoric mammals, like the mastodon.
8000 B.C.–1000 B.C. Archaic Period	Native Americans visited this area seasonally. Fiber-tempered pottery was introduced in the latter part of the period and shell rings like the one in Sea Pines were created.
1000 B.C.–900 A.D. Woodland Period	Native American groups were semi-nomadic, migrating seasonally along river valleys. They hunted animals, such as deer, that would be recognizable today. Crop cultivation began.
900 A.D.–1550 A.D. Mississippian Period	Permanent stratified Native American

settlements began appearing, with crop cultivation and hunting as the means for survival. The groups were Muskegeon speakers, related to the Creeks.

1335 A.D.   Green's Shell Enclosure, a 4-foot-tall shell ridge that encloses 2 acres, was built along the banks of Skull Creek.

European Explorers
1500–1700

1521   A Spanish expedition, led by Francisco Cordillo, explored this area, marking the beginning of the colonization era and initiating European contact with local tribes.

1526   The Spanish established a short-lived settlement called San Miguel de Gualdape on South Carolina's coast. Its 500 colonists were led by Gov. Lucas Vasquez deAllyon.

1562   The French Huguenots, led by Jean Ribaut, entered Port Royal Sound and established Charlesfort on Parris Island. Ribaut left the area and tried to return to France. He was captured off the English coast. The settlers that he had left behind built a ship and also attempted a return to France. They were captured as well. Theirs was the first Protestant settlement in the United States. The Spanish burned it in 1564 after it had already been abandoned.

1566   Spanish explorers settled Santa Elena, a permanent settlement, on Parris Island. They abandoned it in 1587 because British corsairs and Sir Francis Drake had been attacking their holdings in St. Augustine. Then, the Spanish concentrated their colonization efforts in St. Augustine.

1663   Capt. William Hilton sailed from Barbados, on the *Adventure*, to explore lands granted by King Charles II to the eight Lords Proprietors. Hilton Head Island takes its name from a headland near the entrance to Port Royal Sound.

1670   Charles Towne was established by the English on the bank of the Ashley River. The settlement moved to its current location on the peninsula between the Ashley and Cooper Rivers by the 1680s.

1684   The Yemassee Indians began moving into the Port Royal area. They were invited by the Scots who had established Stuart Town. In 1686, the Spanish destroyed Stuart Town.

1698   John Bayley, of Ireland, was given most of Hilton Head Island as a barony. Twenty-four years later, his son appointed Alexander Trench as his agent in charge of selling the land. For a short time, Hilton Head was called Trench's Island on some 18th-century maps.

Plantation Era
1700–1860

1707   A military post was established on the Beaufort River to stop Spanish attacks on Charleston (originally called Charles Towne).

1711   Beaufort, South Carolina, was founded.

1715   Yemassee Indians, in response to abuse by white traders and fearing possible enslavement, attacked several settlements in the Carolinas. They killed many traders and their families. These raids continued for 15 years. The Yemassee were pushed to Florida.

1715   Col. Alexander Mackay settled on what became known as Pinckney Island. The family sold it to Charles Pinckney in 1734. The entire island became a Wildlife Refuge in 1975.

1717	As a reward for his leadership in the Yemassee War, Col. John ("Tuscarora Jack") Barnwell was granted 1,000 acres of land (Myrtle Bank Plantation) on the northwest corner of the island by the Lords Proprietors. He became the island's first white settler. Myrtle Bank is now part of Hilton Head Plantation.
1728	In January, an entire crew of South Carolina scouts was killed by Yemassee Indians on the southern tip of Daufuskie Island, giving the area the name Bloody Point. In March, Col. John Palmer retaliated by attacking St. Augustine, ending most of the Yemassee attacks.
1733	Savannah was founded by James Oglethorpe. It was intended to provide a barrier between Spanish Florida and British Carolina.
1740s	Eliza Lucas introduced a successful strain of indigo that could be grown on the sea islands. She sold the seeds to her father's plantation-owning friends. By the 1750s, most sea island plantations grew indigo. Indigo's cultivation and processing demanded a large amount of slave labor. The end product, bricks of dye, was sold to the English for dyeing fabrics.
1748	The Royal Indigo Bounty was passed by England, making indigo profitable for South Carolinian planters
1760s	Beaufort County's shipbuilding industry was one of the largest in the 13 colonies. The deep-water creeks around Hilton Head and the prevalence of hardwoods (like live oak) made the island a popular place for shipbuilding. Robert Watts constructed the largest ship built in colonial South Carolina on Hilton Head Island; it weighed 420 tons. The USS *Constitution*, "Old Ironsides," was rebuilt in 1997 using live oaks felled during construction of Hilton Head Island's Cross Island Parkway.
1767	St. Luke's Parish, which included Hilton Head Island, became a new colonial parish (a religious and political boundary) due to population growth in the area.
1775	The American Revolution began and England ceased paying a bounty on South Carolina indigo.
1778	The English captured Savannah, Georgia.
1779	Privateers sailing with the British navy burned many houses on Skull Creek and around the island on their way to Beaufort and Charleston. Hilton Head residents tended to be Patriots, while Daufuskie residents were Tories.
1781	Daufuskie Islanders burned several Hilton Head homes, including the Talbird home. A few days later, Philip Martinangele, of Daufuskie Island, led a raiding party to Hilton Head Island, where they killed Charles Davant. The attack was avenged by Capt. John Leacraft and the "Bloody Legion," which went to Daufuskie and killed Martinangele.
1783	The English abandoned Charleston in August.
1788	The Zion Chapel of Ease, a small wooden Episcopal church (40 feet by 20 feet) for plantation owners, was constructed. All that remains is the cemetery, which is home to the Baynard Mausoleum near Mathews Drive.
1790	William Elliott II, of Myrtle Bank Plantation, grew the first successful crop of long-staple, or Sea Island, cotton in South Carolina on Hilton Head Island. Its value was several times that of short-staple inland cotton.
1804	A hurricane passed through this area, killing 500 in South Carolina.
1813	During the War of 1812, British forces landed on Hilton Head Island, burning many of the houses along Skull Creek.
1820s	Some planters began building summer homes where Bluffton is located today. The town was not incorporated until 1852.
1836	Rev. Joseph J. Lawton tried to grow rice on Calibogue Plantation in what is now Sea Pines Plantation. The endeavor failed due to lack of freshwater to flood the fields.
1854	The Church of the Cross was constructed in Bluffton.
1860	There were more than 20 working plantations on the island before the Civil War. Because of the island's isolation and the prevalence of diseases, such as yellow fever

and malaria, most plantation owners did not live on Hilton Head. Instead, they had homes in Charleston, Beaufort, or Savannah. The island was populated with slaves and overseers.

The Civil War and the Union Occupation
1860–1865

1860	In December, South Carolina was the first state to secede from the Union.
1861	On April 12th, the Civil War's first shots were fired on Fort Sumter in Charleston harbor.
1861	Beginning in July, Fort Walker was built on Hilton Head Island at the entrance to Port Royal Sound in order to protect the port from Union attacks.
1861	On November 7th, Union forces attacked Fort Walker (later renamed Fort Welles in honor of Gideon Welles, secretary of the Navy) and Fort Beauregard (across the Port Royal Sound on Bay Point) in the Battle of Port Royal. The naval flotilla consisted of 17 warships, 33 transports, and 25 colliers. Nearly 13,000 Union troops flooded onto the island in the days after the battle. The troops built a pier for warships, and constructed all of the installation's warehouses, sawmills, residences, and its hospital shortly after arriving.
1862	Hilton Head Island was also referred to as Port Royal, in reference to the military installation by that name. Port Royal was the home to the Department of the South.
1862	Hilton Head's population swelled to over 40,000, including Union troops, civilian store-keepers, missionaries, prisoners of war, and slaves seeking refuge from their owners.
1862	Gen. Ormsby Mitchel set up the town of Mitchelville to house the island's contraband community; this was the first freedman's village. Until 1863, slaves were called "contrabands of war" and were considered abandoned property of the plantation owners. Mitchelville residents elected their own officials, passed their own laws, and established the first compulsory education law in the state. The Mitchelville community was built along modern-day Beach City Road.
1862	Northern missionaries participated in the "Port Royal Experiment," which created contraband schools. Penn School, on St. Helena Island, was one of the original schools.
1862	Fort Mitchel was built as a battery to protect Skull Creek from Confederate attacks. Fort Sherman, which circled the military installation, was completed.
1863	On January 1st, President Lincoln signed the Emancipation Proclamation.
1863	Many Bluffton homes were bombarded by Union ships patrolling the May River.
1863	The United States government bought many abandoned plantations at tax sales. Not all of the confiscated property was sold or divided among the freedmen.
1864	In response to decreasing numbers of troops on the island, Fort Howell was constructed by the 32nd U.S. Colored Infantry. It was built on the southwestern side of Mitchelville and is still located along Beach City Road.
1864	Clara Barton, founder of the Red Cross, spent nine months on Hilton Head Island.
1865	On February 1st, President Lincoln signed the 13th Amendment to end slavery.
1865	On April 9th, Gen. Robert E. Lee surrendered to Gen. Ulysses S. Grant at Appomattox. Within two months, the Civil War was over.
1865	The First African Baptist Church was founded in August. Rev. Abraham Murchison of Savannah was the first pastor. Several island churches formed out of this church, including St. James, Goodwill, Central Oakgrove, and Mt. Calvary.
1865	In December, the 13th Amendment was ratified and all slaves were legally freed.

Reconstruction and Isolation
1870s–1940s

1868   Large-scale military occupation of the island had ended. The island's population dropped to only a few thousand. Island residents continued a life of isolation from the mainland. They depended upon subsistence farming, fishing, and oystering to make a living.

1868   Rachel Crane Mather started a school in Beaufort for daughters of freed slaves which became a normal school for black girls in 1882. In 1932, it was approved by the SC Department of Education as an industrial school and opened to all races. It then received accreditation by the Southern Association of Colleges and Schools in 1955. In 1969, it was transferred to the jurisdiction of Beaufort County. It finally became the Technical College of the Low Country (TLC) in 1972 with a branch on Hilton Head Island, which opened in August 1983.

1870s   Some of Hilton Head Island's plantations were reclaimed by their antebellum owners after paying back taxes charged to their property. Other properties were held by the United States government, sold to speculators, or sold to freedmen who remained on the island after the Civil War.

1872   The island was once again referred to as Hilton Head Island instead of Port Royal.

1881   A hurricane killed 700 in South Carolina and Georgia.

1890   William P. Clyde, of New York, bought 9,000 acres of land on Hilton Head Island from former plantation owners and land speculators. Like many other Northern buyers, Clyde used the land for a private hunting preserve.

1891   Savannah State College was founded. Many of Hilton Head Island's residents attended this college. An island native, Cyrus Wiley, graduated from Savannah State in 1899 and returned to the college in 1921 as its second president. He was the first graduate of the college to hold that position. He served as president until 1926.

1893   An enormous hurricane hit Beaufort County, killing at least 2,000 people in the county and flooding parts of the island with its 12-foot surge. Many of Hilton Head Island's structures were destroyed in this storm.

1900s   Private hunting groups, such as the North Carolina Hunting Club, also purchased large sections of Hilton Head Island during this period.

1901   A 15-inch steam cannon was installed and tested on the beach at Coggins Point (modern-day Port Royal Plantation). It was 1 of 13 designed to protect the United States coast.

1917   Troops were stationed at the former Union Fort Walker during World War I as lookouts for possible submarine attacks.

1920s   Gullah native islanders sailed bateaux from Hilton Head to the mainland, carrying people, crops, and livestock to the market on River Street in Savannah. Charlie Simmons Sr. operated the first mechanized ferry in 1930 from Simmons Fish Camp, located near Marshland Road. The *Lola*, a 30-foot boat with a 15-horsepower engine, ran three times a week. The last ferry, the *Alligator*, was larger, quicker, and ran more frequently.

1920s   Many families augmented their incomes by oystering. The Hudsons and Toomers operated oyster factories on Hilton Head from the 1890s until the 1950s. By this time, the boll weevil had destroyed almost all of the Sea Island Cotton in the region.

1930   Landon K. Thorne and Alfred L. Loomis bought W.P. Clyde's and Roy Rainey's properties totaling nearly 20,000 acres for approximately $6 an acre. They had already purchased the former Union Fort Walker from the United States government in 1927. Alfred Mose Hudson served as the woodsrider, or manager, of the property.

1940   The island's population was approximately 1,100, most of whom were descendants from freedmen who had made their homes on Hilton Head. A great storm hit the island, leaving many people stranded and damaging many of the island's structures. Charlie Simmons's 55-foot-long Edgar Hurst ferry was pushed across Broad Creek and onto dry land during this hurricane.

1941   Marines were stationed at Camp McDougal near the Leamington Lighthouse in present-day Palmetto Dunes. The lighthouse had been built in the 1870s and was known as the Hilton Head Lighthouse until the Palmetto Dunes development, Leamington, began. Marines paved the first road on the island, which ran from the ferry landing at Jenkins Island (now Outdoor Resorts) to the lighthouse.

1948   On June 30th, President Harry Truman signed a resolution creating "National Freedom Day" to be celebrated on February 1st. The day was intended to commemorate the signing of the 13th Amendment, which ended slavery. In 1997, a group of Hilton Head Islanders revived National Freedom Day with a Gullah celebration at Simmons Fish Camp.

Mainland Connection and Modern Era
1949–1990s

1949   A group of lumber associates from Hinesville, Georgia, bought a total of 20,000 acres of pine forest on Hilton Head's southern end for an average of nearly $60 an acre. They formed The Hilton Head Company to handle the timber operation. The associates were Gen. Joseph B. Fraser, Fred C. Hack, Olin T. McIntosh, and C.C. Stebbins.

1950   Logging took place on 19,000 acres of the island. There were three lumbermills built to harvest the timber. The island population was only 300 residents.

1950   The first electricity was brought to the island by Palmetto Electric Cooperative. The poles were brought by barge to the island.

1953   A state-operated car ferry began running from Buckingham Landing (near Bluffton, on the mainland) to Jenkins Island (at Outdoor Resorts). The first ferry, the Gay Times, held only four cars. The second one, Pocahontas, held nine. The cost to ride was 10¢ as a pedestrian and $1.25 for a car.

1954   Hilton Head Elementary School opened for the island's black students near the present-day intersection of Wildhorse Road and Highway 278. Prior to this period, students studied in small one- or two-room neighborhood schools that were scattered around the island. Isaac Wilborn was the principal of the elementary school from 1954 until it closed in 1974. The site is now owned by the Town of Hilton Head Island. The school was replaced by a new integrated school constructed on a new site in 1975.

1955   Beaufort county state representative Wilton Graves opened the Sea Crest Motel on Forest Beach. At first, it consisted of two rooms. It expanded to eight by 1960. The first vacation cottages were developed on Folly Field Road, which had been acquired from The Hilton Head Company.

1955   Katie McElveen opened the Roadside Restaurant along Highway 278. It was torn down in 1986 to build Parkway Medical Center.

1956   James F. Byrnes Bridge, a two-lane swing-bridge, was constructed at a cost of $1.5 million. This opened the island to automobile traffic from the mainland, at a $2.50 round-trip toll. Forty-eight thousand cars traveled across the bridge in 1956. The toll was discontinued in December 1959.

1956   Gen. J.B. Fraser withdrew from The Hilton Head Company. His son, Charles E. Fraser, bought his interest and began developing it into Sea Pines Plantation.

1956   Norris and Lois Richardson opened the first supermarket on the island. It was located near Coligny Circle in the North Forest Beach area. Before then, island residents depended upon small, neighborhood general stores to provide for their needs, or they traveled to Savannah.

1956   The Hilton Head Island Chamber of Commerce was established.

1958   First deed to a lot in Sea Pines Plantation was signed. Beachfront lots initially sold for $5,350. By 1962, they were selling for $9,600.

1958   The first year of telephone service was offered by Hargray Telephone Company. Their first Hilton Head office did not open until 1960.

1958   Palmetto Bay Marina opened.

1959   William Hilton Inn opened with 56 rooms. It was torn down to build the Marriott Grand Ocean resort on South Forest Beach Drive in the 1990s.

1959   Hurricane Gracie hit the island causing slight damage.

1959   Organized mosquito spraying began.

1960   The island's first golf course, the Ocean Course, designed by George Cobb, was built in Sea Pines Plantation.

1961   The McIntosh family subdivided 360 acres of The Hilton Head Company to start Spanish Wells.

1962   Port Royal Plantation was developed by Hilton Head Company, led by Fred Hack.

1964   Hilton Head's first condominiums were completed in Sea Pines Plantation.

1964   The Bank of Beaufort began offering banking services on the island for a few hours each week (Monday, Wednesday, and Friday from 10 a.m.–12 p.m. and Tuesday, Thursday from 9 a.m.–9:15 a.m.).

1965   The Sea Pines Medical Center was built. It was staffed by a retired doctor who lived in Sea Pines but served the entire island community.

1965   Hilton Head Island had its first rural mail route established with Phil Propst as the carrier. There were 415 deliveries on the island.

1965   The Women's Association of Hilton Head Island was established. Mrs. Fred C. Hack was the first president.

1965   Sea Pines Academy began. In 1967, the younger students began to be taught in the Montessori manner. In 1986, Sea Pines and May River Academies combined to form Hilton Head Preparatory School.

1967   Sea Pines Plantation installed the island's first gates. Port Royal, Shipyard, and future developments followed the trend.

1967   The Palmetto Dunes area was acquired from the Hilton Head Agricultural Company by the newly formed Palmetto Dunes Corporation, headed by William T. Gregory, for $1,000 an acre.

1967   The Hilton Head Airport opened. The first plane to land belonged to golfer Arnold Palmer.

1968   Sea Pines Montessori School and Sea Pines Academy opened.

1968   Hudson's restaurant was opened by J.B. Hudson Jr.

1969   Harbour Town village was completed. The full-time population of the island was 2,500.

1969   The first Heritage Golf Classic played at Sea Pines's Harbour Town Links. The German firm Badische Anilin and Soda Fabrik (BASF) announced plans for a $100-million chemical plant 3 miles from Hilton Head Island on Victoria Bluff; now the area is a 1,200-acre wildlife refuge and home to the Waddell Mariculture Center.

1970   A group of islanders effectively stopped the development of the BASF chemical plant on the mainland. The island's shrimping co-op, made up of native islanders, played a central role in halting the chemical plant's development. The co-op had over 125 members who operated 30 boats from its dock on Skull Creek (now Skull Creek Seafood). David Jones, head of the cooperative, took his shrimp boat up to Washington to deliver petitions against BASF's plant to Secretary of the Interior Walter Hickel.

1970	*Island Packet* newspaper was first published.
1970	Deep Well Project began.
1970	The Hilton Head Company started Shipyard Plantation.
1971	Sea Pines acquired land on the north end of the island, which was developed into Hilton Head Plantation.
1972	The first movie theater opened on Hilton Head Island in Coligny Plaza. Walt Disney's *Song of the South* was the first movie shown.
1972	Chicago Bridge and Iron (CBI) announced plans to build off-shore drilling platforms on Victoria Bluff.
1973	Moss Creek, the first off-island planned development, began. Rose Hill, Callawassie, Belfair, Colleton River, and others followed in the next 20 years.
1974	The swing-bridge was struck by a barge which forced island residents to travel off the island on a pontoon bridge constructed by the Army Corps of Engineers. The bridge was closed for six weeks.
1975	The island's full-time population by this time was 6,500. Over 250,000 visitors came to Hilton Head.
1975	Hilton Head Hospital was completed.
1975	Time-share condominiums started being sold in Sea Pines.
1975	Pinckney Island's owners, Edward Starr and James Barker, donated their 5,000-acre island to the U.S. Fish and Wildlife Service for conservation.
1975	Hilton Head National Bank opened. It was the first locally owned and operated financial institution on the island.
1979	Hurricane David missed the island, but high winds left beaches eroded and destroyed several Singleton Beach homes.
1982	A four-lane bridge was built to replace the two-lane swing-bridge to the island. The island's full-time population was 12,500. More than 500,000 visitors came to Hilton Head in 1982.
1982	Wexford Plantation and Long Cove Club were developed.
1983	The Town of Hilton Head Island incorporated as a municipality. The town agreed to provide planning services to Hilton Head Island. The first mayor, Ben Racusin, and the town council were elected to two-year terms.
1985	Hilton Head's Comprehensive Plan was adopted by the town council. The population was over 17,000 full-time residents.
1985	Lot sales at Indigo Run began.
1987	The town council passed the Land Management Ordinance of the Town of Hilton Head Island.
1989	Using some state funding, town officials implemented a beach nourishment plan to restore heavily eroded beaches by pumping sand from offshore (repeated in 1997).
1990	The Cross-Island Parkway project was approved. The Parkway's bridge spans Broad Creek and links the south end of the island to the north end.
1991	The Town of Hilton Head Island updated its Comprehensive Plan.
1992	The Beach Preservation Fee (part of Hilton Head Island's 2% Accommodations Tax) was passed by the town council to provide funding for future beach renourishment.
1993	Del Webb Corporation began its 5,100-acre development of Sun City Hilton Head, a retirement community 9 miles west of the island.
1994	Coastal Discovery Museum, formerly the Museum of Hilton Head, and the Hilton Head Chamber of Commerce Welcome Center moved into a shared building along Jarvis Creek at the north end of the island.
1995	The permanent year-round population exceeded 28,000 people. The island had over 1.5 million visitors.
1995	Construction on the Cross-Island Parkway began.
1996	The Master Land Use Plan for Ward One was started by the Town.

1996	Self Family Arts Center opened.
1997	Crossings Park, near the Palmetto Bay Road entrance to the Cross Island Parkway, opened.
1997	The Town of Hilton Head Island began its second update of the Comprehensive Plan.
1997	First Gullah Celebration sponsored by the Native Island Business and Community Association was held.
1998	Cross Island Parkway opened in January. The total cost was $81 million for construction, land acquisition, and planning.

One

IN THE EARLY DAYS

Hilton Head Island's first full-time residents were Native Americans. Occupation of the island has been dated back to at least 2000 B.C. at the Sea Pines Shell Ring. The Yemassee Indians hunted and farmed in this area until the early 18th century. This engraving depicts some Yemassee men burning out a tree in order to make a canoe. Dozens of Native American archaeological sites have been studied and excavated on Hilton Head Island. (Coastal Discovery Museum.)

In 1663, Capt. William Hilton sailed from Barbados on the *Adventure* to explore lands granted by King Charles II of England to the eight Lords Proprietors. Hilton Head Island takes its name from a headland near the entrance to Port Royal Sound named for Captain Hilton. In his journal, Hilton called the island "very pleasant and delightful." Walter Greer, an island artist, painted this image of the *Adventure*, which hangs in the Adventure Inn. (Adventure Inn.)

The plantation era on Hilton Head Island began later than it did near Charleston. This island was not suited for growing rice and was populated with Yemassee Indians. The Stoney-Baynard Ruins in Sea Pines are evidence of early plantation owners. The one-story-and-a-half structure was made of tabby, a mixture of oyster shells, lime (burned oyster shells), sand, and water. Tabby was poured into forms much like cement. (CDM.)

In 1788, a small wooden Episcopal church (40 feet by 20 feet) called the Zion Chapel of Ease was constructed on this property. All that remains is the cemetery, which is home to the Baynard Mausoleum (in the background). The Hilton Head Historical Society owns and protects this property, which is located at the corner of Mathews Drive and William Hilton Parkway. (Ned McNair.)

By 1860, there were more than 20 working plantations on the island. Because of the island's isolation and the prevalence of diseases, such as yellow fever and malaria, most plantation owners did not live on Hilton Head. Instead, they had homes in Charleston, Beaufort, or Savannah. The island was populated with slaves and overseers. Sea Island Cotton was the major source of income for planters owning land on the island. The Fish Haul plantation, also known as Drayton's plantation, is shown here. The slave row consisted of two rows of five houses. Houses were built of wood and had two rooms. Today, only the tabby chimneys of these structures remain. This photograph was taken during the Union occupation of the island. A soldier stands to the right-hand side of the photo. (Western Reserve Historical Society.)

After the Civil War and the Union occupation of Hilton Head ended, the island became extremely isolated. Many wealthy Northerners, such as William P. Clyde, purchased former plantations. In 1890, Clyde bought 9,000 acres of land on Hilton Head Island. Clyde (in the front row, right of center) used the land for a private hunting preserve. (Fred C. Hack family.)

The Hudson family first came to Hilton Head Island in the late 19th century. James Ransom Hudson and his wife, Isabelle, began a long family tradition in the seafood industry. Eventually, the Hudson family (and other families such as the Toomers and Maggionis) operated oyster factories and shrimp-packing houses on Hilton Head. (Propst family.)

21

Coiled baskets are a well-known art form on the sea islands. Basket makers like Caesar Johnson made work baskets out of bulrush and palmetto in forms similar to West African baskets. These three baskets were made by Beaulah Grant Kellerson in 1969. (Abe Grant.)

Honey Horn Plantation was used as a Sea Island Cotton plantation prior to the Civil War. Part of the main house at Honey Horn dates to this period. From the 1890s until the 1950s, hunters such as W.P. Clyde and others used the property as a private hunting reserve. In 1950, the Hack family moved to the property. Fred C. Hack was one of several partners involved in harvesting the island's timber. Later, Hack developed thousands of acres on the island. (Hack family.)

Two

UNDER THE GUN

Since 1861, Hilton Head Island has often been used as military headquarters and for coastal defense. After the Battle of Port Royal Sound on November 7, 1861, Hilton Head (also called Port Royal from 1861 to 1865) was the headquarters for the Union's Department of the South. The T-Dock was the center of the military installation. Ships delivered fresh troops, letters from home, and supplies to the island. The installation was located in what is now Port Royal Plantation. (CDM-Library of Congress.)

Members of the 3rd New Hampshire Regiment Band were a few of the nearly 30,000 Union troops living on the island from 1861 to 1865. These men decorated their living area with a few items picked up along the beach. Whelk shells and palmetto fronds are scattered in front of the tent. (CDM-Library of Congress.)

In 1901, a pneumatic dynamite sea coast gun was built at Coggins Point (present-day Port Royal). The gun, also called the "Steam Cannon," was placed on the island for defense during the Spanish-American War. The barrel of the gun was 15 inches wide and 50 feet long. It was tested over a hundred times, but was never fired on the enemy. The barrel was melted down in World War I. All that remains today are the boilers, concrete housings, and the gun turret (seen here). (Evelyn Mitchell.)

The Hilton Head Lighthouse was originally built by the Coast Guard in the 1870s. This lighthouse was built nearly 1 mile inland, and a smaller range lighthouse was built closer to the beach. Now, it is called the Leamington Lighthouse and is no longer used for navigation. (Parris Island Museum.)

This building was originally adjacent to the Leamington Lighthouse. It was likely used as the keeper's house. After many years of neglect, the building and another one from the property were moved to the Harbour Town village in Sea Pines. They are currently commercial buildings and have been completely refurbished. (CDM.)

Beginning in 1937, the Marine Corps began developing the lighthouse reservation into an advanced training camp for anti-aircraft units and defense battalions. Shown here in 1940, Camp McDougal consisted of barracks, a mess hall, a hospital, an exchange, a recreation room, a boiler and hot water house, ammunition shelters, vehicle sheds, a headquarters building, a pump house, and a water tower. The first unit assigned to Camp McDougal was the 2nd Anti-Aircraft Battalion, which occupied the base beginning in May 1938. The Marines used Camp McDougal throughout World War II for training men—in addition to horses and dogs. (Parris Island Museum.)

The Marines at Camp McDougal were trained to use 5-inch naval guns. This particular gun had a name, "Big Betsy." It was located on the beach approximately 1 mile from the camp. (Barbara Hudson.)

When they were not learning how to use this 3-inch anti-aircraft gun, this group of Marines found out that it made a good perch. (Barbara Hudson.)

Hilton Head also had other anti-aircraft guns, as well as .50- and .30-caliber machine guns. The emplacements of these guns could be seen on the beach many years later. After completing training at Camp McDougal, many battalions were sent overseas. The 3rd was sent to Pearl Harbor, the 2nd to Samoa, and the 4th to Cuba. (Parris Island Museum.)

This Marine truck travels down one of the many unpaved roads on the island during the 1940s. The first paving that was done on the island, though, was done by the Marine Corps. When supplies were brought to the island, they were left at Jenkins Island, which is several miles away from McDougal. The Marines paved the road from the ferry landing to Camp McDougal. (CDM.)

In their spare time, many of the Marines watched boxing matches at outdoor rings, which were constructed near the lighthouse. (Barbara Hudson.)

A small corps of musicians entertained the Marines at Camp McDougal in 1942. This group was called the Hilton Head Orchestra and was made up of only five members. (Barbara Hudson.)

These four Marines stand in front of one of the only stores on the island in the 1940s. Mose Hudson ran this store located near the Jenkins Island ferry dock. The Hudson store was not just a place to purchase necessities, it also became a popular spot for socializing. (Barbara Hudson.)

Three

FRUIT OF THE SEA

After the Civil War, Hilton Head Island was a very peaceful and isolated place. For survival, island residents depended upon what they could grow, catch, or hunt. Surrounded by water, Hilton Head has always been closely associated with the sea. For islanders, oystering, shrimping, crabbing, and fishing have been an important part of life. *Oyster Mist* by Gullah artist Joe Pinckney depicts an oysterman steering his oyster-filled bateau back to land. (Joe Pinckney.)

For decades, oystermen have depended upon harvesting oysters from area waterways for survival during the oyster season (from September to April). Picking oysters was (and is) almost always done by men. Oystermen land their boats on the oyster rakes and gather the oysters using tongs as well as their hands. The work is muddy and can be dangerous. Oyster shells are very sharp and can easily cut unprotected hands. (*Island Packet*.)

Once the oysters were loaded into the bateaux, they were taken to the oyster factories and piled onto large tables. From the 1920s until the 1970s, several island families operated oyster factories. In the Hudson factory, over 250 gallons of oysters were shucked each day by the women working there. Workers were paid with Hudson money, which could only be used at the Hudson store. (Barbara Hudson.)

One of the most popular Lowcountry pastimes is the oyster roast. Such a roast can feed hundreds or just a few like this one after a hunting expedition in the early 1950s. (CDM.)

In 1971, the Hack family hosted an oyster roast at Honey Horn. Mrs. N. Owings, Orion Hack, Nathaniel Owings, Fred C. Hack, M.L. Galston, and Dr. William Odum surround a table full of the local specialty. Mr. Owings and his team researched and reported on the future of the island's environment for The Hilton Head Company. (Hack family.)

Shrimp boats are a common sight around Hilton Head Island's waterways. For generations, families have been harvesting shrimp in the area. Ben Stewart's trawler, the *Captain Ben*, is typical of the modern shrimp boat. (Ben Stewart.)

Shrimpers work long and hard hours. Usually, they leave the dock before dawn and return when the boat is full. Large trawling nets are dragged behind the boats to collect the shrimp. Other fish and sea creatures are also caught. The entire catch is sorted, and unwanted fish are tossed overboard to eagerly awaiting birds and dolphins. (*Island Packet.*)

Many shrimpers sell their catch to seafood processors, who will in turn sell the shrimp to distributors or sell it retail. Here, two young women are removing the heads, called "heading shrimp," to package them and sell at the market. (Elizabeth Grant.)

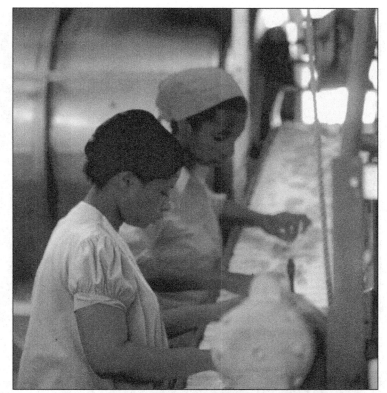

Hilton Head Island is home to a few large-scale shrimping operations such as Benny Hudson Seafood on Squire Pope Road. Shrimpers often sell their catch directly to the dock. In the 1960s and 1970s, a Hilton Head Fisherman's Co-op operated just up the road from Hudson's. The group's 125 members helped fight a chemical plant planned for Victoria Bluff in 1970. (CDM.)

Helen Bryan is one of the only remaining cast net makers on Hilton Head Island. In the past, it was very common for people to produce handmade nets. She hand ties each knot in the net, which is used for catching fish and shrimp. (*Island Packet*-Jay Karr.)

At the Folly, Ronald Williams and Lester Carr demonstrate the proper technique for cast netting. The outside of the net is weighted with metal weights. To cast the net the thrower holds one weight in his teeth and swings the rest of the net out, not forgetting to let go of the weight between his teeth. The weights keep the net open until it reaches the bottom of the water when it can be slowly drawn closed and pulled back up. (*Island Packet*-Jeff Sanford.)

In 1969, Robert Graves, an island resident and home builder, built his first sport fishing boat on Hilton Head Island. The *Versa-Lou* was the first of many luxury watercrafts that Graves and his team constructed near Arrow Road. The *Drumbeat* was towed down Highway 278 in May of 1976. Graves's boats were known to be well built and sturdy. (Abe Grant.)

During the 1970s, Mose Hudson and his pickup truck were a common sight around Hilton Head Island. Mose enjoyed fishing with his family. After a long day of catching, he sold the fish out of his makeshift market, his truck. (Propst family.)

Seafood has long been a part of Hilton Head Island's history. Residents caught and sold fish, oysters, and shrimp for income, but they also kept some for dinner. Today, island residents and visitors alike can be observed picking up some dinner in the waterways by crabbing. The Folly, the tidal inlet creek shown above, is a particularly popular spot. Small cages baited with chicken necks are effective. Both blue and stone crabs can be caught around Hilton Head Island. Novices beware, however, for both varieties can pinch, so be careful. (*Island Packet*-Brian LaPeter.)

Four

FRUIT OF THE LAND

From the 1700s until the middle of the 1900s, Hilton Head Island's economy was agriculturally based. Indigo and cotton were the two plantation-era crops. After the Civil War, small family farms cropped up across the island. Families depended upon what they could grow for food and some income. Vegetable stands are still common sights around the Lowcountry, where vendors sell locally grown produce. (*Island Packet.*)

In the 1740s, indigo was introduced to the sea islands as a cash crop which grew well in sandy soil and in a hot climate. The plant, used to make a deep blue dye, was grown in Africa as a complement to rice. Since Hilton Head did not have enough fresh water to flood rice fields, indigo became the first successful crop grown on the island. In 1748, England passed the Royal Indigo Bounty making indigo profitable for South Carolinian planters. (CDM.)

Saxon Vats were an important tool in the production of indigo dye. Indigo stems and water were placed in the top Saxon Vat and stirred together. Then, the liquid was transferred to the bottom vat, where it was beaten more. The middle vat held water and crushed oyster shell, which was added to bring the dye particles out of solution. After drying the particles out, bricks of dye were formed and sold to the English for dyeing fabrics. (John Monkaitis Model-CDM.)

In 1790, William Elliott II grew the first successful crop of long-staple, or Sea Island, cotton in South Carolina at Myrtle Bank Plantation on Hilton Head Island. Its value was several times that of short-staple inland cotton. Plantation owners became extremely wealthy from Sea Island Cotton. They lived in Charleston, Savannah, or Beaufort to avoid the diseases and climate on the sea islands. (CDM.)

Slaves and overseers were the only full-time residents of Hilton Head prior to the Civil War. This photograph shows a cotton field during the Union occupation of the island. A soldier is standing on the right side, while nearly a dozen contrabands (abandoned slaves) prepare this field for planting. (Western Reserve Historical Society.)

When family groups began farming Hilton Head Island in the late 19th century, they had to grow enough food to support the entire family. There was little opportunity to purchase extra supplies. Tomatoes, potatoes, watermelon, sugar cane, squash, peas, butterbeans, citrus fruit, and numerous other crops were grown on the island for nearly a century. Most of the work had to be done by hand or with limited animal power even through the 1950s when this photo was taken. (Elizabeth Grant.)

Michael Cohen was photographed in 1988 with his Marsh Tackies. These small horses were once common on Hilton Head but are few in number today. According to local legend, the sturdy yet small horses are descended from horses left on the island by the Spanish in the 16th century. These animals were often the only transportation that a family possessed. (*Island Packet.*)

Roy Neil and Bill Taylor of C & D Farms planted tomatoes and other crops on the island from 1953 until 1968. They leased 250 acres from the Hack family for one of the island's largest commercial farms. In other parts of Beaufort County, truck farming was commonplace as early as the 1920s. With no easy way to or from Hilton Head Island before the ferry in 1953, this island was not desirable for truck farmers. The VanDuyn interests also farmed commercially on the island, but they grew gladioli and iris. (Hack family.)

Small family markets such as Gertrude Grant's vegetable market on Highway 278 can still be found around the island. In the past, farmers grew enough to feed their families and then sold any excess. Before the population of Hilton Head grew, most farmers took their excess produce to the Savannah market, as there were not enough customers on Hilton Head Island. (*Island Packet*-Jay Karr.)

Eddie Grant's property on Squire Pope Road was used for several decades as a general store where people bought whatever they could not grow themselves. The Hudsons operated it in the 1920s and then sold it to Mr. Grant, who continued to run a store out of the building. The rest of the acreage has been turned back into a family-run farm and market operated by Eddie Grant. (CDM.)

Vidalia onions, grown in nearby Georgia, used to be available in only a few locations. One such place was the "Onion Man's" school bus. During onion season, he parked the bus in a vacant lot near the corner of Arrow Road and Highway 278 and sold bags of Vidalia onions. For many years, his bus was a regular stop for many visitors and island residents alike. (*Island Packet-*Robert Carlton.)

Heritage Farm in Sea Pines is tended to by members who lease plots of land for their own personal gardens. In 1990, a partnership between the Heritage Farm Organization and the Deep Well Project made pounds of vegetables available to needy families on the island. The Deep Well Project was founded by Charlotte Heinrichs in 1973 to finance bringing clean water to island residents. More recently, its mission includes helping anyone in need of basic necessities. (*Island Packet*-Jeff Sanford.)

Bill Baldwin, a former president of the Heritage Farm Organization, stands in his garden. Plots are 40 feet square and are rented to members. Vegetable and flower gardens cover this property, and dedicated members care for them. The Hilton Head Plantation Farmers Club operates in a similar manner. (CDM.)

Five

IN THE WOODS

From the 1890s through the 1950s, Hilton Head was visited in the winter season by hunting parties searching for game. The Clydes, Hurleys, Thornes, and Loomises used parts of the island as private retreats. Turkey, quail, doves, duck, and other wild fowl were prevalent. Deer, mink, wild boar, alligators, and occasionally, snakes were also the hunters' targets. Will Clyde stands with his guide, Tommy Wright, who shows off the rattlesnake that Clyde hunted. (Hack family.)

Will Clyde and a guest stand on a boat which is navigated through the marsh by two guides. The hunters are looking for water moccasins. Often, Clyde parties went out into the island on carts pulled by horses. Guests were housed at the Honey Horn Plantation house. Mr. J.E. Lawrence was the superintendent of Mr. Clyde's 9,000 acres. (Hack family.)

Mr. J.E. Lawrence, daughter Margaret, his wife, and an unknown companion accompanied Agnes Lucille Hubbard (one of the island's teachers) on a horseback hunt in 1920. Honey Horn had stables of horses for hunters to use. (Elaine Kennedy.)

In 1920, the Hurley family purchased over 1,000 acres on Broad Creek for a personal hunting retreat. W.L. Hurley, a wealthy furniture manufacturer of Philadelphia, often brought his wife, seen here on horseback, down to the island during the winter months. (CDM.)

In 1921, the Hurleys built this large home at Otter Hole Plantation. The home had several bedrooms and fireplaces to keep visitors warm in the winter. The Hurleys brought other luxuries to the island as well. Their yacht was anchored near the house in Broad Creek, and it is said that they had one of the first automobiles on the island. (CDM.)

In the early 1930s, the Hurley estate sold Otter Hole to Landon K. Thorne and Alfred L. Loomis. The Priesters lived at Otter Hole and worked for Thorne and Loomis. A member of the Priester family stands in front of the home built by the Hurleys. From this view, the size of the house is clear. Later occupants of the home include Miss Milley, island postmistress, and a nightclub from 1972 until the building burned down in 1974. (Lamar Priester Jr.)

Lamar Priester Sr. and his son, Lamar Jr., stand next to the Otter Hole house steps. Lamar Sr. was the huntmaster at the Honey Horn property, owned by Thorne and Loomis. The family remained on the island until Lamar Jr. was of school age, at which point they moved to the mainland. (Lamar Priester Jr.)

Lamar Priester rode his horse, Blackjack, through thousands of acres of Hilton Head Island during his short stay. He recalled that very important guests such as the king of Sweden were often included in the Thorne and Loomis parties. (Lamar Priester Jr.)

In 1917, a group of North Carolina hunters began buying property near present-day Palmetto Dunes for a hunting lodge. They amassed 2,000 acres and called themselves the Hilton Head Agricultural Club because they intended to grow limited amounts of cotton. Their agricultural pursuits were unsuccessful. By the 1930s, there were over 40 members associated through business and family connections. Some Chattanoogans were also included, although the core group of members came from near Gastonia, North Carolina. This photograph was taken in front of the clubhouse during the 1939 hunt. Members met in Savannah for an annual banquet and then rode the *Clivedon*, the ferry, to Hilton Head the next morning. (Charles S. Thompson (CST) scrapbook.)

Frank B. Thompson, Mark K. Wilson, and Charles S. Thompson are seated in front of the clubhouse on the Hilton Head Agricultural Club's property. The hunt weeks on Hilton Head were full of camaraderie and reunions. Charles S. Thompson, on the right, was one of the original founders of the club. (CST scrapbook.)

On some occasions, Hilton Head Agricultural Club members brought their families along for the fun. These children posed next to one of the day's trophies; they are, from left to right, as follows: (front row) Mary K. Winget and Anna Boyce Rankin; (back row) Bob Van Sleen, Margaret McConnell, Tom Thompson, and Grady Rankin. (CST scrapbook.)

Jake Brown and his wife stand next to one of the Hilton Head Agricultural Club's cabins in 1928. Brown, a native of Hilton Head Island, was the manager of the property for many years. (CST scrapbook.)

Several cabins, like this one shown in 1939, served as the hunters' accommodations. Staying on Hilton Head Island in the 1920s and 1930s was not luxurious, but it was comfortable. (CST scrapbook.)

As a young man in the 1930s, Mose Hudson acted as the woodsrider for the Thorne and Loomis property. By then, they owned nearly 20,000 acres of the island. Hudson scoured the woods on horseback keeping trespassing hunters away and making sure that the reserve was well stocked with mink and other game. Sometimes, he trapped rattlesnakes to sell their venom to vendors in Savannah. Hudson had been born on the island in 1905 and knew his way around the island as well as anyone. (Propst family.)

After the Hack family purchased Honey Horn plantation in 1950, hunting parties continued. Guests stayed on the Honey Horn property and went on guided hunts. Richard Chisholm, on the left, was one of the guides. (CDM.)

From the 1940s to the early 1960s, Curtis Thompson and his hunting dogs came down to Hilton Head Island from North Carolina for the hunting season. He stayed on the Honey Horn property. (CDM.)

Six

LIVING AND LEARNING

Hilton Head Island's schools and churches have always played a part in educating the island's population. Over the past century, the size, number, and variety of schools and churches have evolved. In the early part of this century, one-room schoolhouses dotted the island's landscape, and there were only a handful of churches in which to worship. Today, there are more students than ever in the schools and dozens of churches for islanders to attend. (Elaine Kennedy.)

From 1919 to 1922, Agnes Lucille Hubbard taught a total of 42 white children in the Honey Horn School. The school was under supervision of the Bluffton public school system. The building, formerly located on the Honey Horn property, had one room and a wood stove heater. (Elaine Kennedy.)

Until the 1970s, Hilton Head Island's black students attended separate schools. There were nearly half a dozen one-room schoolhouses serving island neighborhoods. The Cherry Hill schoolhouse was built in 1933 on Beach City Road. Beaufort County paid teachers to come to Hilton Head only three months out of the year. Parents often pooled resources to keep teachers at the schools for an additional month. Most children needed to work with their families when school was not in session. (CDM.)

The Robinson Middle School was one of the largest schools for African Americans on the island before the 1950s. Students could attend classes up to the middle grades in this building. In order for children to continue their education, families had to send them to boarding schools like the Penn or Mather School in Beaufort or children had to live with relatives in Savannah. (Ed Wiggins Sr.)

In the 1950s, Honey Horn was still being used by white children. Aileen McGinty (left of center) was photographed in 1955 with her four students, from left to right, Frederick Hack Jr., Dianne Taylor, Avary Hack, and F. Gracie Hodges. Byron Hack, in the front, was visiting his brother and sister that day. This small group of students put on plays and took a lot of field trips. Mrs. McGinty arranged with the Savannah library to allow her to check out three books per student per week. (Hack family.)

M.C. Riley School in Bluffton graduated its first 12th-grade class in 1954. After that, Hilton Head Island students could travel to Bluffton to complete the 12th grade. Delores Brown-Lawyer was the 1962 valedictorian at M.C. Riley. Here she poses with her diploma inside the auditorium. (Delores Lawyer.)

Prom night at M.C. Riley brought students together to celebrate their upcoming graduation. James Wiley, Anne Cooke, Delores Brown-Lawyer, Lee Smalls, Delores Bryant-Anderson, and Michael Heyward posed together in 1962. (Delores Lawyer.)

In 1954, Hilton Head Elementary School opened for the island's black students. The school's construction was part of the state's School Expansion Program from 1951 to 1954. With seven classrooms and a cafeteria/auditorium, this was the largest school ever built on the island. Integration of the school was mandatory in 1972. Isaac Wilborn was this school's only principal, serving from 1954 until 1974, when the school closed because it was replaced with a larger, new school. The building was used for a county courthouse annex for a few years and was torn down in the early 1990s. (*Island Packet*-Brian LaPeter.)

The Children's Center was chartered in 1967 as the Child Youth Development Center. Several island residents, including Isaac Wilborn and Art Hedemenn, recognized a need for affordable day care for families. The day care was first housed in a rented building on Mathews Drive until its current building was completed in 1969. (*Island Packet*.)

One of the oldest structures on the island, the Queen Chapel, A.M.E. Church is located on Beach City Road. African Methodist-Episcopal missionaries founded the Queen Chapel in 1865. The original building had been a praise house used by slaves on the Pope plantation. The structure was updated in 1892 and 1952. (CDM.)

The St. James Baptist Church, at the corner of Dillon and Beach City Roads, was organized in August 1886. Its location is adjacent to the Mitchelville neighborhood, where contrabands (abandoned slaves) farmed land during the Civil War. St. James owns the Cherry Hill schoolhouse and uses it for church activities. (Delores Lawyer.)

The First African Baptist Church, located on Beach City Road, was founded in August 1865. Rev. Abraham Murchison of Savannah was its first pastor. Several island churches formed from this church, including St. James, Goodwill, Central Oakgrove, and Mt. Calvary. (Delores Lawyer.)

Central Oak Grove Church on Mathews Drive was photographed before its new steeple was added. The home behind it is no longer standing. (*Island Packet.*)

Mount Calvary Church was organized in 1914 on property donated by Katie Miller. The church operates a preschool in the back of the building, which is on Squire Pope Road. (Delores Lawyer.)

Rev. Benjamin Williams of Mount Calvary Church occasionally holds baptisms in the waters of Skull Creek. This custom used to be widespread but has not been practiced as much recently. Williams is only the fifth pastor at the church. (Greg Smith.)

This little chapel on the Honey Horn property was used from the 1930s until 1957. Charleston Presbytery sent a student minister, Mills J.Peebles, to serve as minister in the chapel in the spring and summer of 1957. He became the first pastor of the First Presbyterian Church of Hilton Head when it was established in November 1957. Recently, the chapel was moved to the First Presbyterian Church property on Highway 278 near Mathews Drive. (Hack family.)

The First Presbyterian Church congregation moved from Honey Horn into its new location in 1965. It was built on 5.5 acres donated by Fred C. Hack Sr. and Olin T. McIntosh. The church has been expanded many times since then. (First Presbyterian Church.)

The early 1960s and 1970s marked the beginning of a wave of church construction on the island. Several churches were built along Pope Avenue to cater to the expanding population of Sea Pines and the rest of the island. The First Baptist, shown here, was built in 1965 on South Forest Beach Road. Also, the construction of St. Luke's Episcopal began in 1964. Other church groups, including United Methodist, gathered wherever they could, often at the William Hilton Inn. (Ernest Ferguson.)

The 1971 groundbreaking mass for the Church Holy Family took place in 1971. Bishop Ernest Unterkoefler led the mass while Bobby Cole, John Capin, and Charlie Dean assisted. Many other congregations had similar outdoor services in the 1960s and 1970s as the population of the island continued to grow. (Capin family.)

Seven

WAY TO GO!

Mose Hudson and his son, Lynn, stand on the ferry dock at Jenkins Island. Before the bridge was built to connect Hilton Head to the mainland, the island remained isolated. Transportation after arriving on the island was challenging too. Roads were not paved and were often too small for vehicles. Over the years, access to the island has become much easier. (Propst family.)

Regular ferry service kept Hilton Head Islanders connected to the mainland in the early 1900s. The *Clivedon* was one ferry which ran until the late 1930s. The captain navigated this steamship from the bridge seen here. On the top deck, with his elbow on the rail, is Captain Polite. (Barbara Hudson.)

The *Clivedon* was originally built in 1890 to carry freight. After a short period, it was refitted as a passenger ferry. It ran from Savannah to Beaufort, stopping on Daufuskie and Hilton Head. The *Clivedon* was one of several ferries stopping at the Jenkins Island dock, which made it easier for island residents to travel around the area and for hunting parties to enjoy their retreats. (CST scrapbook.)

One of the most common sights around Hilton Head Island prior to the 1960s was the bateau. This model shows the sail-powered bateau that was used by islanders to make trips to Savannah. Often, they were loaded with produce to sell in the market. Later, owners added engines to these boats making the trip to Savannah much quicker. Solomon Campbell was one of the last bateau builders on the island. He fashioned cypress planks into bateaux in a variety of sizes. (Seymour Lash Model-CDM photo.)

Starting in 1930, islanders had another way to get to Savannah. Charlie Simmons purchased the *Lola*, a mechanized boat, in 1930. Over the next 25 years, he owned several ferries which he used to take people, the mail, produce, livestock, or anything else from Hilton Head to Savannah and back. The *Alligator*, seen here unloading timber workers at the Jenkins Island dock, was Mr. Simmons's last boat. (Hack family.)

In 1953, Mose Hudson operated the first state-run ferry to Hilton Head. The first ferry, the *Gay Times*, carried only four cars. It was actually a barge that was pushed across the water from Buckingham Landing to Jenkins Island. Here, Hudson is photographed on the *Pocahontas*, the second ferry. On his right are crates of tomatoes from the C & D truck farm located on the island. (Propst family.)

The *Pocahontas* held nine cars and was operated until 1956. Five times a day the ferry traveled across Skull Creek from Buckingham Landing to Jenkins Island. It cost 10¢ for a pedestrian and $1.25 for a car to ride on the ferry. (CDM.)

Before the car ferry, it was very rare to have an automobile on the island. The Hurleys are supposed to have been the first ones to have a car on the island. By 1930, Lamar Priester Sr. did have an early model Ford on the roads. Priester was the manager of the Honey Horn property for the Thornes and Loomises. (Lamar Priester Jr.)

The Hudson brothers, T.C. and J.B., pose against another of the vehicles on the island. In 1940, there were only a dozen cars on the island. It is said that residents recognized the sounds of each car and always knew who was coming before they arrived. (Barbara Hudson.)

The J. Byrnes Bridge opened on May 20, 1956. A crowd gathered for the ceremonies and then traveled to the Honey Horn property for a celebration. This was the first bridge connecting Hilton Head to the mainland. The cost was $1.5 million. (CDM.)

In its first year, 48,000 cars crossed the bridge. At first, the bridge cost $2.50 per round trip. The toll was phased out by 1959. The Byrnes Bridge was a swing bridge. It swung open to allow boats to pass through on either side of the center support. (Ernest Ferguson.)

In 1974, the swing-bridge was struck by a barge, which forced island residents to travel off the island on a pontoon bridge constructed by the Army Corps of Engineers. The pontoon bridge was floated into position and opened a few times a day for boat traffic. The swing bridge was closed for six weeks. (Evelyn Mitchell.)

The central control area of the swing bridge was the keeper's house, which was perched at the top of the frame. The bridge tender in the 1980s had a busy job. Right next to the old bridge, the new one was being constructed. (*Island Packet*.)

In 1982, a four-lane stationary bridge was built to replace the two-lane swing bridge to the island. The new bridge is on the right-hand side of this photo. The old bridge was torn down shortly after the J. Wilton Graves (named for a former state representative) Bridge opened. (*Island Packet*.)

This view of Broad Creek shows the Cross Island Parkway Bridge being constructed. Approval for the toll road which connects the north end of the island to the south end came in 1990. The road opened in January 1998. The total cost was $81 million. (*Hilton Head Monthly-Rob Kaufman*.)

With all of the new visitors and residents to the island after the opening of the Byrnes Bridge, many of the roads were paved for the first time. Until the 1950s, Highway 278 (then known as Route 44) was paved from Jenkins Island to Camp McDougal, near present-day Palmetto Dunes. In 1967, the road was renamed Highway 278. The whole road was two lanes until 1977, when it was widened to four lanes. (Hack family.)

In 1967, the Hilton Head Airport opened. There were two airstrips on the island before this one. The first jet to land belonged to golfer Arnold Palmer. In 1969, this aerial photo was taken of the brand-new terminal area. The terminal was an A-frame structure and has been renovated to accommodate private passengers since the new terminal opened across the runway in the 1990s. (Tommy Heyward.)

Possibly the most recognized part of any road on Hilton Head is the Sea Pines Traffic Circle. Completed in 1962, the circle has long been controversial and the object of many a visitor's frustration. This 1992 view shows Highway 278 at the bottom, Palmetto Bay Road on the right, Greenwood Drive at the top, and Pope Avenue to the left. (*Island Packet*-Jay Karr.)

Eight

DEVELOPING HILTON HEAD ISLAND

The Byrnes Bridge's opening marked the beginning of enormous changes on Hilton Head Island. Prior to 1956, the Sea Crest Motel on North Forest Beach was one of the only places to stay. It had two rooms in 1955, but had expanded to eight by 1960. A handful of new residents relocated to Hilton Head before 1956, but activity increased once access to the island improved. This aerial view shows North Forest Beach and the Coligny Circle in the 1960s. (Ernest Ferguson.)

Several beach cottages had been built in the Folly Field neighborhood before the bridge. Many families purchased these homes to use for vacation retreats. (Hack family.)

Port Royal Plantation began being developed in 1962. This aerial view is of the Grasslawn area near the modern-day Westin Resort. This piece of property at the "heel" of Hilton Head Island contained Fort Walker, Fort Sherman, and the Steam Cannon. The Hilton Head Company, led by Fred C. Hack Sr., made efforts to preserve these historic sites. (Hack family.)

Sea Pines Plantation was possibly the island's best-known development in the 1950s and 1960s. In 1956, Charles Fraser bought his father's interest in The Hilton Head Company and began planning and building a 5,000-acre residential development. In 1958, the first lot sold. Oceanfront lots initially sold for $5,350. By 1960, these same lots sold for $9,600. In the early years, this gate marked the entrance to Sea Pines. (Frances Baker.)

Fraser's intention was to develop a year-round residential area with all the amenities that families wanted. As for recreation, golf course designer George Cobb was hired to build the Ocean Course in 1960. The clubhouse followed shortly afterwards and included a pro shop and eventually a dining room. (Frances Baker.)

Houses in Sea Pines were designed to fit into the landscape. One of the major concerns for developing the area was that the environment should be protected. Sea Pines planned a number of nature reserve areas including the Forest Preserve, which is several hundred acres. Sea Pines president Charles Fraser won nationwide recognition and the American Institute of Architects' 1968 "Citation for Excellence in Private Community Planning" for his land planning and development methods. (CDM.)

Some of the most innovative and interesting buildings in Sea Pines are hidden in the woods behind Harbour Town. The Sea Lofts, also called Treehouses, were designed by Bertoli in the early 1970s. (CDM.)

The striped lighthouse at Harbour Town may be one of the island's most recognizable symbols today, but, in 1968, the area looked very different. Beginning in July 1968, over 250,000 cubic yards of earth were dredged from the Harbour Town site. By the time this photograph was taken, 2,592 feet of concrete bulkheading had been installed around the 6-acre harbor. (Ed Pinckney and Associates.)

In the 1970s, Sea Pines added another marina to the property. South Beach Marina resembles a New England harbor town and is located at the southernmost "toe" of the island. (Ernest Ferguson.)

The William Hilton Inn opened in 1959 and hosted many of Sea Pines's visitors. Initially, it had 56 rooms but was eventually expanded to 80. The Sea Pines Company owned and operated the inn for many years. (Ernest Ferguson.)

Hilton Head Island's beautiful beaches brought many visitors to the island. Elizabeth Grant visited the island and then moved here in the 1960s. Once she moved here, Elizabeth was very active in painting and drawing. (Elizabeth Grant.)

The William Hilton Inn's pool was also a favorite spot for guests. The inn had activities planned throughout the year. The evenings were full of activities as well. Dining and entertainment were always popular. (Ernest Ferguson.)

An additional hotel opened in May 1963. The Adventure Inn had 45 rooms initially. By 1969, Hilton Head was attracting conventions, like this one, from around the country. In 1972, the governors' convention was held on the island. Conferences and groups continue to schedule meetings on Hilton Head to enjoy the island's offerings. (Adventure Inn.)

The Port Royal Inn and golf club were located at the opposite end of the island. The golf club was constructed in 1965. The Barony and Robbers Row golf courses were added amenities on Port Royal's property. (Hack family.)

Built in 1964, the Port Royal Inn had 44 rooms and additional villas available for visitors and conferences to use. The inn was burned down in 1973 and was not rebuilt. (Hack family.)

The Westin Resort is located adjacent to Port Royal. It is one of the largest resort hotels on the island. It was originally built as an Inter-Continental Hotel. (The Westin Resort.)

In 1967, the Palmetto Dunes Corporation purchased the Hilton Head Agricultural Company's holdings. The cost was nearly $1,000 an acre. During the 1970s, the area began to be developed. The Hyatt, in the center, opened in 1976. Several condominium buildings and villas were built later. (*Island Packet*-Brian LaPeter.)

In 1970, The Hilton Head Company began planning the Shipyard property. Eleven years later, the Marriott Resort opened. It operated from 1981 until 1992. After a $6.6-million renovation, the Crystal Sands reopened in March 1993 as the Crowne Plaza Resort. (Crowne Plaza.)

The Holiday Inn was built in 1971 on South Forest Beach Drive. It has 200 rooms and an oceanfront pool. The South Forest Beach area near the hotel has many oceanfront condominiums which are visible from this aerial view. (Ernest Ferguson.)

The Hilton Resort opened in February 1983. Originally called the Mariner's Inn, the Hilton took over the property in 1992. The hotel is in Palmetto Dunes. (CDM.)

The Marriott Grande Ocean Resort's first phase was completed in 1993. The property that it occupies was once the site of the William Hilton Inn, which was demolished after 30 years on the beach. The Marriott Grande Ocean is one of several Marriott timeshares built around the island. (*Island Packet*-Jay Karr.)

After ten years of planning and building at the Palmetto Dunes Resort, Shelter Cove Harbor began to be a reality in 1981. Across Highway 278 from Palmetto Dunes, the harbor is located on Broad Creek. (*Island Packet.*)

By 1996, Shelter Cove Harbor had a much different appearance. Disney's Hilton Head Island Resort occupies the 15-acre island. The property has over 100 rooms and villas for members to use. The resort also has access to a beach club in Palmetto Dunes. (Disney's Hilton Head Island Resort.)

Nine

A GROWING COMMUNITY

As the population of Hilton Head Island grew from the 1950s on, community services and modern conveniences increased as well. Services that had been extremely rare or non-existent before became readily available on the sea island. One of those modern conveniences was electricity. The Palmetto Electric Cooperative had an office in Ridgeland when the officers decided to extend power lines to the island in 1950. The Ridgeland staff posed in front of the office in the early 1950s. They are, from left to right, as follows: (front row) Jep Smith, "Preacher" Cope, Willie Padgett, Archie Davis, Grayson Cope, and Edison Smith; (second row) Frank Cordrey, Betty Smith, Jennie V. Smith, Carrie Wells, and Frances Huguenin. (Palmetto Electric Cooperative.)

Prior to 1950, electricity was not available on the island. In its first year of operation, Palmetto Electric Cooperative served 89 members, and they noted that there could possibly be 146 other members. The poles were brought over on barges, as neither the ferry nor the bridge was yet an option for travel. The company completed installing the lines over the Intracoastal Waterway in 1951. Palmetto Electric Cooperative contracted to open its first Hilton Head office in 1958. (Palmetto Electric Cooperative.)

Telephone service followed a few years after electrical service. In 1958, Hargray Telephone Company began serving customers on Hilton Head Island. The office did not open until 1960. Shown here in 1973, Hargray's headquarters was manned 24 hours a day. (*Island Packet.*)

This post office was constructed in 1953 near Wild Horse Road on Highway 278. Miss Beatrice Milley was the island's postmistress from 1942 until 1963. Miss Milley knew everyone on the island when she took her position. Islanders came to pick up their mail at the post office. A replacement for this post office was constructed nearby when the volume of mail increased on the island. (*Island Packet.*)

In 1965, the island had its first rural mail route established. Phil Propst, seen here, was the first rural carrier on the island. He delivered mail to over 400 residences and businesses. Six years later, a second route was organized. Propst became the superintendent of postal operations on the island in the late 1970s. (Propst family.)

In 1975, the Hilton Head Medial Center and Clinics opened on land donated by the Palmetto Dunes Resort. All of the nurses were on hand for the opening ceremonies. Before then, island residents had few options when seeking medical assistance. In the early years, there were several residents who understood and used natural medicines. Families usually depended upon midwives to deliver babies. A small health clinic near Sea Pines opened in 1965. It was staffed by a retired doctor and was open to all of the island's residents. (Hilton Head Medical Center and Clinics.)

After many years of being serviced by the Beaufort County Bookmobile, Hilton Head Island's first library opened in February 1969. Mrs. William Patterson was the first director of the branch, which was housed in an expanding mobile home on Highway 278. The library cost $14,000 to be constructed. (*Island Packet.*)

The Bargain Box opened in 1965 at the intersection of Folly Field Road and Highway 278. This thrift shop was operated by Mrs. Fred Wilkins, Mrs. David Williamson, and Mrs. Fred C. Hack. Its first mission was to raise funds for the First Presbyterian Church building fund. Later, the mission used the funds provided by selling household goods at low cost to needy patrons to operate a grant-funding organization which donates thousands of dollars each year to island charities and non-profit organizations. Today, the shop is located on the grounds of the First Presbyterian Church. (*Island Packet.*)

The community of Hilton Head continued to grow in the 1970s when many cultural groups were formed. Art exhibits became more frequent as galleries opened. In 1970, Elizabeth Grant displayed some of her artwork at the First Presbyterian Church. Standing next to her are Mr. and Mrs. Fred C. Hack Sr. (on the right) and Frederick Hack Jr. (on the left). (Hack family.)

In 1973, Dana Palmer, an island artist, lived for a while in this bread truck at the Palmetto Bay Marina. His family ran the Red Piano Gallery on Cordillo Parkway. (Dana Palmer.)

At the same marina, nearly 25 years later, an Art League group gathered for an outing. (June Eggert.)

The Community Playhouse, as the Hilton Head Playhouse was called in 1977, was the only place to experience the theater on Hilton Head Island. Prior to its construction, drama groups performed at hotels. (Self Family Arts Center.)

The Hilton Head Community Orchestra is one of several musical groups that have been formed over the past several decades. (*Island Packet.*)

In 1996, the Community Playhouse and the Cultural Council combined efforts to form the Self Family Arts Center. The Self family donated funding and land for the construction of the Arts Center, which opened near Shelter Cove Harbor in 1996. (Self Family Arts Center.)

After nearly 30 years of growth on Hilton Head Island, the Town of Hilton Head was incorporated in 1983. In April 1992, town offices moved to the current location near Wexford Plantation. The Island Barbershoppers entertained those who attended the opening. (*Island Packet*-Brian LaPeter.)

Festivals and celebrations have become a big part of Hilton Head Island life. The Saint Patrick's Day parade is one event which draws a large crowd. In the 1998 parade, Sue and Bob Wiener were accompanied by Oscar (the one in the basket), in the Senior Hospitality Activities, Recreation, and Education (SHARE) center's parade entry. (Sue and Bob Wiener.)

The Coastal Discovery Museum, located near the bridge to the mainland, serves island visitors and residents by educating them about the natural and cultural heritage of the island. Originally founded in 1985 as the Museum of Hilton Head, Coastal Discovery offers educational tours and cruises as well as informative exhibits and special events. The museum jointly owns its building with the Hilton Head Island Chamber of Commerce Welcome Center, which also makes it an important stop for island visitors. (CDM.)

Ten

TAKING CARE OF BUSINESS

It is difficult for most visitors to Hilton Head to imagine what the island was like when there were only a handful of restaurants, stores, or hotels to choose from; for hundreds of years, that was the case. It is only recently that amenities have popped up on the island. One of the best-known island businesses is Hudson's Restaurant. In 1968, Benny and Barbara Hudson opened a restaurant adjacent to his family's shrimp docks. The restaurant was one of a few places to have dinner on the island. The restaurant is currently owned by Brian and Gloria Carmines. (Barbara Hudson.)

In 1949, a group of timber associates from Hinesville, Georgia, bought 20,000 acres of pine forest on Hilton Head's southern end. The Hilton Head Company was founded to manage the timber cutting. The four partners were Gen. Joseph B. Fraser, Fred C. Hack, (shown here), Olin T. McIntosh, and C.C. Stebbins. All of the men invested in the island for the timber. After the harvesting was complete, however, these visionaries turned their sights on developing the island. (Hack family.)

From 1950 until 1952, thousands of acres of pine forest were harvested. There were three lumbermills built to process the pines. This one was located near Seabrook Landing on Skull Creek. Since the island population at the time was only a few hundred residents, workers were brought in by boat from the mainland at the beginning of the week and went back to the mainland on the weekends. (Hack family.)

After cutting the timber, the challenge was not complete. Lumber was loaded onto trucks and driven to Possum Point (near modern-day Palmetto Bay Marina). There, barges waited to transport the pine timber to the mainland. (Hack family.)

Island native Abe Grant first operated a store on Highway 278 in 1961. He left the island and moved to Florida for a short time before returning and opening a grocery store in 1965. Grant's store was one of several neighborhood stores operating on the island. In 1968, Grant opened Abe's Restaurant across the street from his store. He also ran a nightclub, the Driftwood Lounge, and pool hall on the same property. (Abe Grant.)

In 1955, Katie McElveen opened the Roadside Restaurant on Highway 278. She operated the restaurant, which featured home-cooked meals, Monday through Friday for 30 years. In 1985, the property was demolished, and the Parkway Medical Center was built. (*Island Packet.*)

Another island institution opened in 1973. Harold's Diner was owned and operated by Harold Smalls. It is located at the corner of Singleton Beach Road and Highway 278. (CDM.)

Down the road from Harold's is the Driessen's Grocery Store and Service Station. Henry Driessen Sr. ran a store on this property as early as the 1920s. In 1950, he built a store next to the current station for his business. In the early 1960s, the Driessen's store and station moved to its present location. The family has continued the tradition; Henry C. Driessen Jr. and his family still run the business. (CDM.)

The Hilton Head National Bank opened on Pope Avenue in 1975. It was the first locally owned and operated financial institution on the island. Before this bank opened, islanders could bank with the Bank of Beaufort, which opened in 1964 at Coligny Plaza. Initially, the bank offered services from 10 a.m.–12 p.m. on Mondays, Wednesdays, and Fridays and from 9 a.m.–9:15 a.m. on Tuesdays and Thursdays. (Elrid Moody.)

Coligny Plaza, the island's first shopping center, began to be built in the early 1960s. By the late 1960s, it had expanded and many island businesses called the center their home. When the Capins moved to the island, they were the first residents of Palmetto Dunes and also the first residents to run a full-service pharmacy. In 1968, Joe Capin and his daughter, Jennifer, stood in front of the new store in Coligny Plaza. (Capin family.)

This building was moved to the island from Ridgeland in 1972. The Bethlehem Baptist Church had a "for sale" sign on it when the Edwards family drove past it in 1972. They purchased it and arranged to move it over land and water to its present location near the entrance of the Long Cove Club, where it houses the Greenery. In the rush to load the church and move it, the movers accidentally forgot the belfry. By the time the Edwards returned to retrieve it, the belfry had been destroyed. (*Island Packet.*)

In 1985, several officials, including Mayor Ben Racusin (left of center), gathered for the groundbreaking of the Gullah Market. The market, at the corner intersection of Squire Pope Road and Highway 278, sells housewares as well as local crafts and produce. Perry White continues to operate the Gullah Market. (*Island Packet*-Brian LaPeter.)

Island Rentals and Real Estate was formed in 1959 to offer rental services to visitors and property management services for part-time residents. The company still maintains some of its original rental properties in Sea Pines. Many of the clients have been renting the same houses for nearly 20 years. In 1989, the office was covered in one of the island's rare snowfalls. (Island Rentals and Real Estate.)

The Hilton Head Island Chamber of Commerce has provided services to island businesses and industries since its founding in 1957. In 1960, the office was in the schoolhouse on the Honey Horn property. The main offices moved near Shelter Cove in 1984, and the Welcome Center for visitors shares a building with the Coastal Discovery Museum near the bridge. (Hilton Head Island Chamber of Commerce.)

Eleven

JUST FOR FUN

Because of the beautiful environment and mild climate, outdoor activities have always been a part of the island's history. While today the island may be best known for its beaches and golf courses, visitors and residents have found numerous other ways to enjoy the beauty of Hilton Head Island. The waterways around the island have supplied food to islanders, but these children do not seem to be catching too much. Just learning how to throw a cast net can be fun. (Disney's Hilton Head Island Resort.)

In the 1920s, horses were the primary means of transportation around the island, but spare time was also spent on horseback. (Elaine Kennedy.)

Ethel Hudson (Propst) found a way to entertain herself in this small boat. During the 1940s, island children played in the woods and waterways when they were not in school. (Propst family.)

Picnics at the beach are a perfect way to enjoy the outdoors. In 1954, Mr. and Mrs. Olin T. McIntosh, Virginia Holmgren, Wallace Martin, Billie Hack, Byron Hack, and Orion Hack gathered at the end of Pope Avenue for an afternoon picnic. (Hack family.)

Hilton Head Island's beaches became a popular day trip for area residents after the Byrnes Bridge opened in 1956. The Arcade opened in 1957 as the Forest Beach Bathhouse. Inside, beach-goers could buy sodas and snacks or they could change into their suits. The McKibben family owned and operated the Arcade. (Marian Broome.)

A very young Tom Peeples enjoys Hilton Head Island's water in 1955. He probably had no idea that the very island he visited would eventually be home to over 30,000 people and that he would be the town's mayor. (Mary Ann Peeples.)

In Sea Pines, the Beach Lagoon house was a popular spot for residents and guests to spend the afternoon. (Ed Pinckney and Associates.)

A few miles up the beach, Gayle and Kim Childers (left and right) spent a vacation at Singleton Beach in 1961. (Betty Lightfoot.)

Arnold Palmer won the inaugural Heritage Golf Classic during Thanksgiving week in 1969. Harbour Town Links was designed by Pete Dye, assisted by Jack Nicklaus. The yet-to-be-finished Harbour Town lighthouse is in the background. The island's first golf course was completed in 1960. After designing the Ocean Course in Sea Pines, George Cobb followed it by building several other courses on the island. (*Island Packet*.)

A Heritage tradition is for the past year's winner to hit the first shot of the tournament while the cannon is fired next to him. This marks the beginning of the tournament. In 1987, MCI Communications took over the Heritage tournament. It was renamed the MCI Classic-The Heritage of Golf in 1994. (Greg Smith.)

Island golf courses are not just for professional golfers. In 1969, football star Fran Tarkington played at Port Royal and enjoyed the island retreat. He is joined by Fred C. Hack and George Cobb, designer for many of Hilton Head's early golf courses. Since the 1960s, there have been over 15 courses built on the island. Golf is enjoyed by many of the island's visitors and year-round residents. (Hack family.)

Beginning in the 1970s, Hilton Head began to be known as a tennis destination. There were courts at the Adventure Inn in the late 1960s. The number of courts on Hilton Head exploded during the island's development. (Adventure Inn.)

In 1973, Dick Butera and Fred C. Hack Sr. of The Hilton Head Company helped tennis professional Billie Jean King break ground for the Hilton Head Surf and Racquet Club. The resort had 20 lighted courts. Pete Collins was the first professional at the club. After several owners and name changes, a well-known tennis pro and teacher purchased the property in 1993. It is called the Shipyard Racquet Club/Van DerMeer Tennis Center. (Hack family.)

Since 1973, the Sea Pines Racquet Club has been the host for the Family Circle Magazine Cup. Rosie Casals, volleying the ball, was the first winner. She and Martina Navratilova (also seen here) teamed together for doubles at one of the early tournaments. (*Island Packet.*)

Since 1989, the Technical College of the Low Country has offered a tennis management program to teach future tennis teachers and professionals. The curriculum includes tennis and business courses and attracts students from all over the world. In the early 1990s, the team was visited by Billie Jean King during the Family Circle Magazine Cup tournament. (Technical College of the Low Country.)

115

For several years, including 1989, Hilton Head Island hosted at triathlon, which started on the beach. Hundreds of participants competed for the title. (Greg Smith.)

Sailing regattas can often be spotted in the waterways surrounding Hilton Head Island. For years, sailing and boating have been favorite pastimes of island residents and visitors. (Ed Pinckney and Associates.)

Beginning in 1968, Gators football became a popular activity for island children. The teams are divided into age groups and garner a great deal of community support. The team shown here lost only one game that season. (Abe Grant.)

At the seasonal polo matches held on the grounds of Honey Horn, the half-time hat competition was popular. Mrs. Charles Perry showed off her creativity with this hat made from cut-out photographs. (Hack family.)

The Hacks hosted polo matches on Honey Horn for three seasons in the 1970s. In the first season, the teams consisted of out-of-towners. Thereafter, a club of U.S. Polo Association members was formed. The competing teams were composed around a nucleus of local players. Games were held on Sunday afternoons, and spectators were charged $1 per car for admission. (Hack family.)

Twelve

Naturally Hilton Head

Hilton Head is a combination of diverse ecosystems, from the beaches to the forests. All of these areas offer exciting opportunities to observe various kinds of wildlife. Hilton Head Island's residents and visitors take pride in the diversity of animals found here and are committed to preserving natural areas as habitats for wildlife. This conservation ethic will ensure that the natural side of Hilton Head Island will be enjoyed by future generations of residents and visitors. One of the most common birds on the island is the ring-billed seagull. They are year-round island residents and can be very friendly, if you have food. (June Eggert.)

While the waterways surrounding Hilton Head once served to isolate and preserve the island, they now offer endless amounts of recreation, from kayaking to sailing and nature cruising. Being a barrier island, Hilton Head has thousands of acres of salt marsh on its land-ward side. Salt marshes are extremely important to the region, acting as a nursery for fish, shellfish, and birds. Marshes also offer protection from flooding by slowly draining rain water. (Ned McNair.)

Many visitors and residents of Hilton Head are drawn to the beach. Hilton Head has approximately 14 miles of beach stretching from Sea Pines to Port Royal Plantations. At low tide, the gradual slope of the sand offers wide expanses for bike riding and beach walking. (Ned McNair.)

Due to the diversity of habitats in the area, a variety of wading, shore, and perching birds can be seen. While Great Blue Herons are commonly found in the salt marshes hunting, they can also be spotted on the beach in the early morning hours. (Gretchen Freund.)

Hilton Head is located in one of the flight paths, called flyways, of migrating birds. Each fall, a number of different raptors, or birds of prey, can be spotted flying over the island. Additionally, many species of hawk, eagle, and others live here year-round. (Sandy Painter.)

While alligators were once an endangered species, they are now common again. Most alligators can be spotted near freshwater ponds and lagoons, but occasionally they are found in salt water, on the beaches, and even in parking lots. Caution must always be used around these animals, as they can be dangerous. (June Eggert.)

From the native marsh tackey workhorses to the riding stables of today, horses have long been part of the Lowcountry's history. This mother and foal were photographed at Lawton Stables in Sea Pines. The island is home to several riding stables. Many people enjoy how Hilton Head looks from atop a horse. (June Eggert.)

Deer are a common sight on Hilton Head. Many residents feel closer to nature when a doe brings her fawn into their yard. (*Island Packet*.)

A seasonal visitor to the beaches is the nationally threatened Loggerhead Sea Turtle. The females' nesting success is monitored each year by the Coastal Discovery Museum's Sea Turtle Protection Project, with support from the Town of Hilton Head Island. The data collected is reported to the South Carolina Department of Natural Resources. Of thousands of hatchlings documented each year, it is estimated that only 1 out of every 10,000 will live to adulthood. (*Island Packet*-Brian LaPeter.)

Bottlenose dolphins are the most common marine mammal of the area. The dolphins of this region are world renowned for their unique feeding behavior called "strand feeding." The dolphins will chase a school of fish onto the mud flats and then beach themselves while snatching up fish. When they are finished, the dolphins slide back into the water. Strand feeding has not been witnessed anywhere else in the world. (Gretchen Freund.)

From June to November each year, Hilton Head watches for hurricanes, such as Hurricane David, which hit Savannah in 1979. The first line of defense against the flooding of a hurricane is the beach and dunes. After Hurricane David, the beach required a massive clean-up effort. (*Island Packet.*)

To protect against hurricane damage, beach renourishment is a technique used to replenish sand that has eroded from the beach. Hilton Head's first renourishment project was in 1990 and was repeated again in 1997. This view toward Burke's and Singleton Beaches shows the pipes used to move the sand from offshore onto the beach. In 1992, the Beach Preservation Fee (part of Hilton Head Island's 2% Accommodations Tax) was passed by the town council to provide funding for future beach renourishment. (*Hilton Head Monthly*-Rob Kaufman.)

Extremes of nature do occur here but not often. Being subtropical in climate means that Hilton Head rarely receives snow, let alone an accumulation as seen here. In February 1968, Byron Hack examined the snowfall on the Port Royal Golf Course. (Hack family.)

Minor flooding may be a fairly common event, but this major flood in October 1994 closed down many roadways. This view down South Forest Beach shows a less common use of a canoe on Hilton Head—paddling home. (*Island Packet*-Jay Karr.)

There are many individuals and clubs devoted to learning more about Hilton Head's environment. The Audubon Society, seen here on a beach walk in 1971, is one of several organized groups that has long held an interest in the natural world of Hilton Head. Hilton Head's Audubon Club began in 1960. Caroline G. ("Beanie") Newhall was the first president and the namesake of the club's preserve on Palmetto Bay Road. The club affiliated with the National Society in 1973. (*Island Packet.*)

Beginning in 1972, controversy exploded in the Lowcountry around Chicago Bridge and Iron's plans to build off-shore drilling platforms on nearby Victoria Bluff. The community had fought off a BASF chemical plant's construction only a couple of years earlier. Boat trips like this one on the *Waving Girl* were organized to show the pristine quality of the area and promote the bluff's conservation. (*Island Packet.*)

The Coastal Discovery Museum is dedicated to preserving the natural and historic wonders of Hilton Head. This is done through educational programs for adults, residents, visitors, and schoolchildren. These youngsters are learning about the salt marsh and marine environments by examining live animals caught in a cast net. (Electric Cooperatives of South Carolina-John Bruce.)

CPSIA information can be obtained
at www.ICGtesting.com
Printed in the USA
LVOW05*1131210817
545790LV00017B/526/P